Paul TAFFANEL

Grand Fantasy

(Grande Fantaisie)
on themes from the opera "Mignon"
by Ambroise Thomas

for Flute and Piano

Edited by
SIR JAMES GALWAY

Paul Taffanel, Grande Fantaisie
(on themes from the opera "Mignon" by Ambroise Thomas)
Performance notes by SIR JAMES GALWAY

This is one of the most played and favorite compositions of Taffanel. There are many editions of this wonderful piece and here I offer you an edition with dynamics and tempi I use when performing the piece in public.

In playing it, I adopt a style more common to singers than to flute players. That is to say, I use a generous tone throughout the piece and concentrate on the breathing.

I have marked the breathing I use and have tried to indicate the *rallentandi* and tempo changes. The breath marks are of two kinds: (✓) being a very quick and short breath whereas (') is a regular breath mark. For a short breath, I would recommend that you don't open your mouth so much but that you acquire the technique of taking a lot of breath through your lips in the embouchure position.

Grande Fantaisie
on themes from the opera "Mignon" by Ambroise Thomas
for Flute and Piano

SU795

Paul Taffanel
edited by Sir James Galway

4

6

SU795

SU795

Digital and photographic copying of this page is illegal.

Paul TAFFANEL

Grand Fantasy

(Grande Fantaisie)
on themes from the opera "Mignon"
by Ambroise Thomas

for Flute and Piano

Edited by
SIR JAMES GALWAY

Paul Taffanel, Grande Fantaisie
(on themes from the opera "Mignon" by Ambroise Thomas)
Performance notes by SIR JAMES GALWAY

This is one of the most played and favorite compositions of Taffanel. There are many editions of this wonderful piece and here I offer you an edition with dynamics and tempi I use when performing the piece in public.

In playing it, I adopt a style more common to singers than to flute players. That is to say, I use a generous tone throughout the piece and concentrate on the breathing.

I have marked the breathing I use and have tried to indicate the *rallentandi* and tempo changes. The breath marks are of two kinds: (✓) being a very quick and short breath whereas (') is a regular breath mark. For a short breath, I would recommend that you don't open your mouth so much but that you acquire the technique of taking a lot of breath through your lips in the embouchure position.

Grande Fantaisie
on themes from the opera "Mignon" by Ambroise Thomas
for Flute and Piano

Flute

Paul Taffanel
edited by Sir James Galway

4

Flute

Flute

Flute

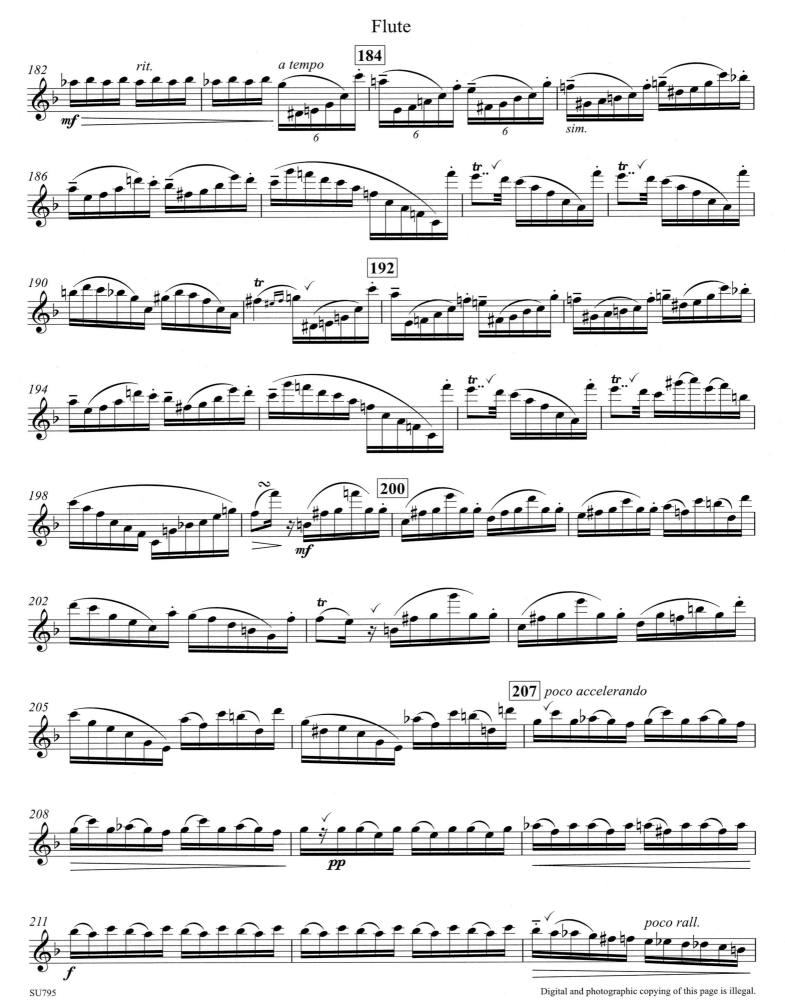

Flute

Flute

Flute

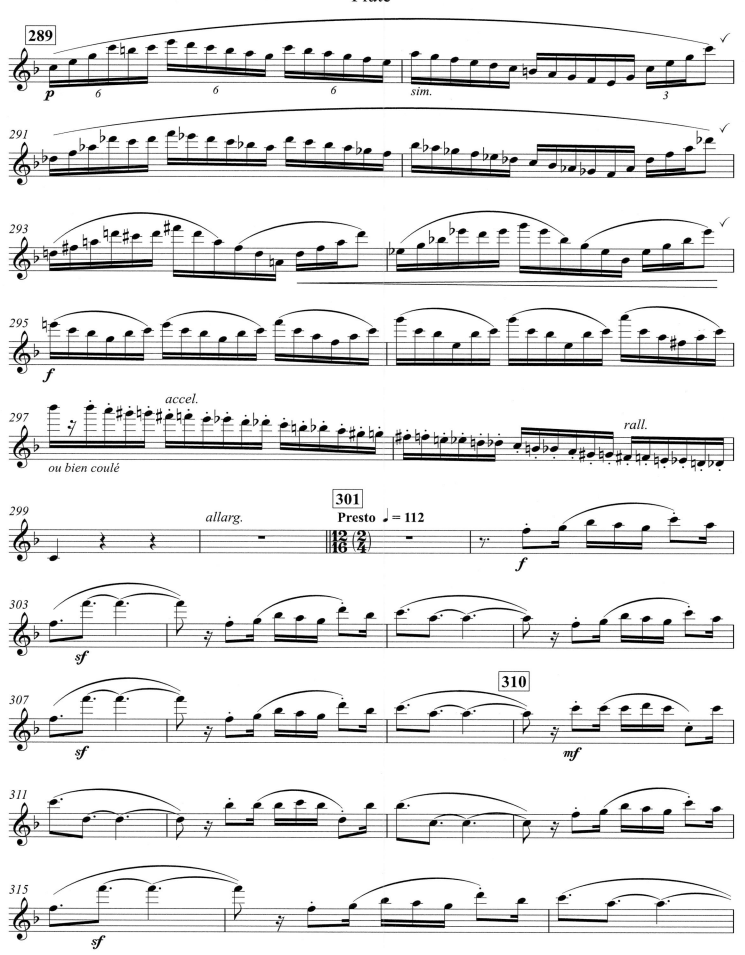

Flute

Flute

Sir James Galway Selected Publications

FLUTE

COLLECTIONS

B579 **Andrew, Nancy-Paris Conservatory Album: 16** HL240976
Short Lyric Pieces for Flute and Piano

This collection is the first-ever publication of 19th-20th Century exam pieces composed for the Paris Conservatory, meticulously compiled, arranged and edited over the course of many years by accomplished flutist Nancy Andrews. All 16 pieces include solo flute part with piano accompaniments. Optional digital downloads are available as well of the original cello/ string ensemble accompaniments where avaialble.

Sir James Galway's introduction to the album states: "It is my great pleasure to present this collection of pieces originally intended as the sight reading exam for the flute class of the Paris conservatoire. Each piece is a little jewel and could be used as an encore to a recital or even in the main part of a recital. Nancy Andrew has done a magnificent job of preparing them for publication. I look forward with great joy to include them in my future recitals."

Works included:

Charles Colin 1873 Allegretto
Ernest Guiraud 1874 Allegretto Scherzando
Emile Paladilhe 1875 Allegretto moderato
Jules Cohen 1878 Andantino
Theodore Dubois 1880 Allegretto
Jules Duprato 1882 Allegro Moderato
Adrien Barthe 1886 Andante
1891 Moderato
1895 Allegretto
Georges Marty 1893 Allegretto
Paul Vidal 1894 Allegro Moderato
Raoul Pugno 1896 Tres doux et tres tranquille
Alphonse Duvernoy 1897 Allegretto
Alphonse Duvernoy 1899 Allegro Moderato
Gabriel Pierne 1918 Modere
Jules Mouquet 1924 Andantino

B577 **Gilbert, W.S. and Sir Arthur Sullivan-Arias for** HL240978
Flute and Piano

Sir James Galway first came upon Gilbert and Sullivan's wonderful operettas while playing with Sadler's Wells Opera orchestra, which later became the English National Opera. His fondness for good tunes, with which the G&S operettas abound, led to this collection, created with longtime collaborator and arranger David Overton.The Gilbert and Sullivan arrangements are divided into separate albums, as some of the songs are best suited to solo flute and piano, some for two flutes and piano, and some lend themselves to a flute choir. This volume for flute and piano contains: • A wand'ring minstrel I (Mikado)• ""On a tree by a river (Mikado)""• Poor wand'ring one (Pirates)• ""Take a pair of sparkling eyes (Gondoliers)""• The flowers that bloom in the spring (Mikado)• The sun whose rays (Mikado)• When a merry maid marries (Gondoliers)

B583 **Gilbert, W.S. and Sir Arthur Sullivan-Arias for** HL240979
Flute Choir

While playing with Sadler's Wells Opera orchestra (later became the English National Opera), Sir James Galway first came upon Gilbert and Sullivan's wonderful operettas. His fondness for good tunes, with which the G&S operettas abound, led to this collection, created with longtime collaborator and arranger David Overton. This volume for flute choir contains: • Brightly dawns our wedding day (Mikado)• For he's gone and married Yum-Yum (Mikado)• I am a courtier, crave and serious (Gondoliers)• Strephon's a Member of Parliament (Iolanthe)

B584 **Gilbert, W.S. and Sir Arthur Sullivan-Arias for** HL240981
Two Flutes and Piano

Sir James Galway first came upon Gilbert and Sullivan's wonderful operettas while playing with Sadler's Wells Opera orchestra, which later became the English National Opera. This album for two flutes and piano, created with longtime collaborator and arranger David Overton contains: • Dance a Cachucha (Gondoliers)• If we're week enough to tarry (Iolanthe)• None shall part us (Iolanthe)• We're called Gondolieri (Gondoliers)

SOLO, UNACCOMPANIED

SU794 **Reichert, M.A.-The Encore Solo** HL240984

Sir James Galway became acquainted with this short but brilliant encore of Reichert's while visiting Albert K. Cooper at his home in south London. This new exclusive edition presents the work as performed by James Galway himself.

SOLO WITH PIANO

SU797 **Briccialdi, Giulio-The Carnival of Venice (Il** HL240977
Carnevale di Venezia)

This exclusive edition of Carnival of Venice (Il Carnevale di Venezia) for flute and piano is edited, arranged and performed by Sir James Galway, regarded widely as the supreme interpreter of the classical flute repertoire. Giulio Briccialdi (1818-1881) was born in Terni, Italy and studies flute with his father until the age of 14. Following the passing of his father, Briccialdi moved to Rome, where he studied composition and was appointed to the Accademia di Santa Cecilia as flute teacher. He would ultimately go on to teach flute to Italian royalty, including the king's brother. He also toured as a performer throughout Europe and America and finally settled in London becoming a director of the instrument-making firm, Rudall and Rose. Besides the mechanical developments he would pioneer at that company, Briccialdi's virtuoso arrangement of the popular "Carnival of Venice" theme would become one of his most enduring legacies.

SU804 **Mouquet, Jules-La Flute de Pan** HL240982

With an updated flute solo part edited by Sir James Galway, this new publication introduces Mouquet's whimsical work to a new generation of flutists. In 3 movements: I. Pan Et Les Bergers (Pan and the Shepherds), II. Pan Et Les Oiseaux (Pan and the Birds), III. Pan Et Les Nymphes (Pan and the Nymphs)

SU805 **Quantz, Johann Joachim-Concerto in G Major** HL240983

One of the gems of Baroque flute repertoire. Features newly engraved flute part, edited by Sir James Galway.

SU795 **Taffanel, Paul-Grand Fantasy on Mignon** HL240985

Adapted and based on themes from the Ambroise Thomas opera Mignon, this Paul Taffanel work is a firmly established part of the modern flute repertoire. This new Southern publication features Sir James Galway's own phrasing and performance markings in a clean, modern re-engraved flute solo part.

SU798 **Wetzger, Paul-By the Forest Brook (Am** HL240986
Waldesbach), Op. 33

PAUL WETZGER (1870-1937) was a German flutist and composer born in Dahme, near Lübeck. At a young age, he took violin lessons from the local music director, later switching to flute. By 15 years of age, Wetzger had played his first concert in the main church of Dahmen and was second flutist of the municipal orchestra. He later became solo flutist with the municipal orchestra of Essen and taught at the Essen conservatory. He wrote numerous pieces for flute and several chamber music works, also editing works by the French composer/ flutist, Jules Demersseman. Wetzger's "Am Waldesbach" (By the Forest Brook), Idyll for flute and orchestra or piano, was a staple of celebrated flutist Marcel Moyse, recorded by him in 1935 on the French Columbia label. Since then, it has become a favorite in the flute teaching repertory, perhaps most notably included Toshio Takahashi's famous Suzuki Flute Method. This Southern Music edition faithfully captures this classic piece as performed by living legend of the flute, Sir James Galway.

SU803 **Widor, Charles-Marie-Suite** HL240987

Charles-Marie Widor (1844-1937) was a French composer and organist, most remembered for his ten organ symphonies. Flutists however, know him best as the composer of this Suite for Flute and Piano, which has become adopted in the standard flute repertoire. This edition features a newly engraved flute part, edited by Sir James Galway. In four movements: I. (moderato), II. Scherzo, III. Romance, IV. Final

Exclusively distributed by  HAL•LEONARD® CORPORATION

Questions/ comments? info@laurenkeisermusic.com